BITCOIN

EVERYTHING YOU NEED TO KNOW ABOUT THE NEW DIGITAL GOLD

PETER VAN DIJCK

Copyright Notice.

©Peter van Dijck

All rights reserved. No part of this publication may be reproduced, distributed or transmitted by any means or in any form, including but not limited to photocopying, recording, or other electronic or mechanical methods, without the prior written permission of the publisher, except in the case of brief quotations embodied in reviews and certain noncommercial uses acceptable to the copyright law.

Trademarked names appear in an editorial style without trademark symbols accompanying every occurrence of trademark names throughout the eBook. These names are used with no intention to infringe on the copyrights of respective owner trademarks. The information in this book is distributed on an "as is" basis, exclusively for educational purposes, without warranty. Neither the author nor the publisher shall have any liability to any person or entity with respect to any loss or damage caused or alleged to be caused directly or indirectly by the information contained in this book.

By reading this document, the reader agrees that Peter van Dijck is under no circumstances responsible for any losses, direct or indirect, which are incurred as a result of the use of information contained within this document, including, but not limited to, —errors, omissions or inaccuracies.

Table of Contents

CHAPTER 1: INTRODUCTION TO BITCOIN 1

INTRODUCTION 1

DEFINITION OF BITCOIN 1

HOW BITCOIN WORKS 1

Benefits and Risks of Bitcoin 1

How to Make Money with Bitcoin 2

Volatility of Bitcoin 2

World Experiences Bitcoin 3

The Future of Bitcoin 3

How to Setup an Account 4

How Does Bitcoin Work as an Anonymous Payment Processor? 4

HOW DOES BITCOIN WORK AS AN INVESTMENT? 4

Bitcoin Casino and Poker Sites 4

How Do You Send Bitcoin? 5

HOW TO BUY BITCOIN 5

What do you need to know about having a bitcoin wallet on your computer? 6

Where can you buy bitcoin like this? 11

How Not to Buy Bitcoin 13

WHAT MAKES BITCOIN SO VOLATILE? 18

BITCOIN VALUE 21

CHAPTER 2: BITCOIN HISTORY 24

BITCOIN HISTORY 24

Bitcoin Price 24

BitCoin Price - Wild Market Speculators 25

BitCoin Price - Stable Investing and Beyond.. 25

BitCoin Halving - Keeping The Limit 26

BitCoin Halving and BitCoin Mining.. 26

Why BitCoin Halving Is Necessary 26

BitCoin Halving and The BitCoin Community 27

BITCOIN FUTURE TRENDS 30

CHAPTER 3: BITCOIN TRADING.. 32

BITCOIN IMPACT ON CURRENCY 34

CHAPTER 4: BITCOIN IN NUTSHELL.. 36

BITCOIN REALITY 36

Block chain 37

Real meaning 38

CHAPTER 5: BITCOIN WALLET 39

Having a BitCoin Wallet Online. 39

Having a BitCoin Wallet Offline. 40

How to Create A Bitcoin Paper Wallet.. 41

A Currency Powered By an Algorithm 43

Purchasing and Paying In Bitcoins 43

Protect and Secure Your Digital Wallet... 43

CHAPTER 6: BITCOIN EXCHANGE RATE 44

Trading The Bitcoin Exchange Rate 44

The Price Volatility Associated With Bitcoins... 44

Look For Online Reviews Before Buying 45

Independent Digital Wallet Or Bitcoin Exchange Account? 45

When Is The Right Time To Buy? 46

CHAPTER 7: BITCOIN SCAM 47

1. Malware is hidden in fake Bitcoin wallets 48

2. Bitcoin phishing.. 48

3. Bitcoin 'flipping.' 48

4. Pyramid schemes.. 49

Bitcoin Digital Wallet Safety Tips.. 49

CHAPTER 8: BITCOIN USERS 50

Protect Your Secure Password... 50

Do Not Publish Your Bitcoin Address Online 50

Check Your Computer for Spyware... 51

BITCOIN CASINO PLAYER AND MEMPOOL 54

CHAPTER 1: INTRODUCTION TO BITCOIN

INTRODUCTION

Bitcoin has been in the news the last couple of weeks, but a lot of people are still unaware of them. Could Bitcoin be the future of online currency? This is just one of the questions, frequently asked about Bitcoin.

DEFINITION OF BITCOIN

Bitcoin is a type of electronic currency (Crypto-Currency) that is autonomous from traditional banking and came into circulation in 2009. According to some of the top online traders, Bitcoin is considered as the best known digital currency that relies on computer networks to solve complex mathematical problems, to verify and record the details of each transaction made.

HOW BITCOIN WORKS

The Bitcoin exchange rate does not depend on the central bank, and there is no single authority that governs the supply of Crypto-Currency. However, the Bitcoin price depends on the level of confidence its users have, as the more major companies accept Bitcoin as a method of payment, the more successful Bitcoin will become.

Benefits and Risks of Bitcoin

One of the benefits of Bitcoin is its low inflation risk. Traditional currencies suffer from inflation, and they tend to lose their purchasing power each year, as governments continue to use quantitative easing to stimulate the economy.

Bitcoin doesn't suffer from low inflation because Bitcoin mining is limited to just 21 million units. That means the release of new Bitcoins is slowing down and the full amount will be mined out within the next couple of decades. Experts have predicted that the last Bitcoin will be mined by 2050.

Bitcoin has a low risk of collapse, unlike traditional currencies that rely on governments. When currencies collapse, it leads to hyperinflation or the wipeout of one's savings in an instant.

Bitcoin exchange rate is not regulated by any government and is a digital currency available worldwide.

Bitcoin is easy to carry. A billion dollars in the Bitcoin can be stored on a memory stick and placed in one's pocket. It is that easy to transport Bitcoins compared to paper money.

One disadvantage of Bitcoin is its untraceable nature, as Governments and other organisations cannot trace the source of your funds and as such can attract some unscrupulous individuals.

How to Make Money with Bitcoin

Unlike other currencies, there are three ways to make money with Bitcoin, saving, trading and mining. Bitcoin can be traded on open markets, which means you can buy Bitcoin low and sell them high.

Volatility of Bitcoin

The value of Bitcoin dropped in recent weeks because of the abrupt stoppage of trading in Mt. Gox, which is the largest Bitcoin exchange in the world. According to unverified sources, trading was stopped due to malleability-related theft that was said to be worth more than 744,000. The incident has affected the confidence of the investors to the virtual currency.

According to Bitcoin chart, the Bitcoin exchange rate went up to more than $1,100 last December. That was when more people became aware about the digital currency, then the incident with Mt. Gox happened and it dropped to around $530.

In 2014, We expect exponential growth in the popularity of bitcoin around the world with both merchants and consumers, Stephen Pair, BitPay's cofounder and CTO, "and anticipate seeing the biggest growth in China, India, Russia and South America.

India has already been cited as the next likely popular market that Bitcoin could move into. Africa could also benefit hugely from using BTC as a currency-of-exchange to get around not having a functioning central bank system or any other country that relies heavily on mobile payments. Bitcoin's expansion in 2014 will be led by Bitcoin ATMs, mobile apps and tools.

World Experiences Bitcoin

More people have accepted the use of Bitcoin and supporters hope that one day, the digital currency will be used by consumers for their online shopping and other electronic deals. Major companies have already accepted payments using the virtual currency. Some of the large firms include Fiverr, TigerDirect and Zynga, among others.

The Future of Bitcoin

Bitcoin works, but critics have said that the digital currency is not ready to be used by the mainstream because of its volatility. They also point to the hacking of the Bitcoin exchange in the past that has resulted in the loss of several millions of dollars.

Supporters of digital currencies have said that there are newer exchanges that are supervised by financial experts and venture capitalists. Experts added that there is still hope for the virtual currency system and the predicted growth is huge.

Bitcoins are a decentralized form of crypto currency. Meaning, they are not regulated by a financial institution or the government. As such, unlike a traditional bank account, you do not need a long list a paperwork such as an ID in order for you to establish what's known as a bitcoin wallet. The bitcoin wallet is what you will use to access your bitcoins and to send bitcoins to other individuals.

How to Setup an Account

You can acquire a bitcoin wallet from a bitcoin broker such as Coinbase. When you open up a wallet through a certified broker, you are given a bitcoin address which is a series of numbers and letters, similarly to an account number for a bank account and a private key which is a series of numbers and letters as well, which serve as your password.

How Does Bitcoin Work as an Anonymous Payment Processor?

You can do 3 things with bitcoins, you can make a purchase, send money anonymously to someone or utilize it as an investment. More and more merchants have been accepting bitcoins as a form of payment. By utilizing bitcoins instead of cash, you are essentially making that purchase anonymously. The same thing goes for sending money, based on the fact that you do not have to submit a mountain of payment in order for you to establish a bitcoin anonymously, essentially you can send money to someone else anonymously.

HOW DOES BITCOIN WORK AS AN INVESTMENT?

The price of a bitcoin fluctuates from time to time. Just to put things in perspective, back in the beginning of 2013, the average price of a bitcoin was approximately $400 per bitcoin, but by the end of 2013, the price of bitcoin rose to over $1000. This meant that if you had two bitcoins worth $800 at the beginning of 2013 and you stored it as an investment by the end of 2013, those two bitcoins would have been worth over $2000 instead of $800. Many people store bitcoins because the value of it fluctuates.

Bitcoin Casino and Poker Sites

Due to the anonymity of bitcoin, the gambling industry has taken up bitcoin as a payment method. Both bitcoin casinos and bitcoin poker sites are coming to life and offering their players to make deposits, play with bitcoin at the tables and withdraw directly to their bitcoin wallet. This means that there's no taxes or possibilities for government control. Much like a regular Nevada casino where do you don't need to register anywhere, and all your transactions are anonymous.

How Do You Send Bitcoin?

For you to pay for goods and services or to send bitcoins to an individual, three things are needed. Your bitcoin address, your private key and the individual's bitcoin address. From that point, through your Bitcoin wallet, you will put three pieces of information, which are: input, balance and output. Input refers to your address, balance refers to a number of bitcoins you are going to send and output is the recipient's address.

HOW TO BUY BITCOIN

The best way to learn about Bitcoin is to jump in and get a few in your **"pocket"** to get a feel for how they work.

Despite the hype about how difficult and dangerous it can be, getting bitcoins is a lot easier and safer than you might think. In a lot of ways, it is probably easier than opening an account at a traditional bank. And, given what has been happening in the banking system, it is probably safer too.

There are a few things to learn: getting and using a software wallet, learning how to send and receive money, learning how to buy Bitcoin from a person or exchange.

Preparation

Before getting started, you will need to get yourself a wallet. You can do this easily enough by registering with one of the exchanges which will host wallet for you. And, although I think you are going to want to have one or more exchange wallets eventually, you should start with one on your computer both to get a better feel for bitcoin and because the exchanges are still experimental themselves. When we get to that stage of the discussion, I will be advising that you get in the habit of moving your money and coins off the exchanges or diversifying across exchanges to keep your money safe.

BITCOIN

What is a wallet?

It is a way to store your bitcoins. Specifically, it is software that has been designed to store bitcoin. It can be run on your desktop computer, laptop, mobile device (except, as yet, Apple) and can also be made to store bitcoins on things like thumb drives. If you are concerned about being hacked, then that is a good option. Even the **Winklevoss*** twins, who have millions invested in bitcoin, put their investment on hard drives which they then put into a safety deposit box.

*The Winklevoss twins are the ones who originally had the idea for a social networking site that became Facebook. They hired Mark Zuckerberg who took their idea as his own and became immensely rich.

What do you need to know about having a bitcoin wallet on your computer?

Below you can download the original bitcoin wallet, or client, in Windows or Mac format. These are not just wallets but are in fact part of the bitcoin network. They will receive, store, and send your bitcoins. You can create one or more addresses with a click (address is a number that looks like this: 1LyFcQatbg4BvT9gGTz6VdqqHKpPn5QBuk). You will see a field where you can copy and paste a number like this from a person you want to send money to and off it will go directly into that person's wallet. You can even create a QR code which will let someone take a picture with an app on their phone and send you some bitcoin. It is perfectly safe to give these out - the address and QR code are both for my donations page. Feel free to donate!

NOTE: This type of wallet acts both as a wallet for you and as part of the bitcoin system. The reason bitcoin works is that every transaction is broadcast and recorded as a number across the entire system (meaning that every transaction is confirmed and made irreversible by the network itself). Any computer with the right software can be part of that system, checking and supporting the network. This wallet serves as your personal wallet and also as a support for that system. Therefore, be aware that it will take up 8-9 gigabytes of your computer's memory. After you install the wallet, it will take as much as a day for the wallet to sync with the network. This is normal, does not harm your computer, and makes the system as a whole more secure, so it's a good idea.

Bitcoin Qt

- The original wallet.
- This is a full-featured wallet: create multiple addresses to receive bitcoins, send bitcoins easily, track transactions, and back up your wallet.
- Outside of the time, it takes to sync; this is a very easy to use option.
- Search for Bitcoin-Qt wallet download to find their site.

Armory

- Runs on top of Bitcoin Qt, so it has all of the same syncing requirements.
- Armoury allows you to back up, encrypt, and the ability to store your bitcoins off the line.
- Search for Bitcoin Armory Wallet to find their site.

If you don't want to have that much memory used or don't want to wait for your wallet to sync, there are good wallets that do not make you sync the entire history of bitcoin:

Multibit

- A lightweight wallet that syncs quickly. This is very good for new users.
- Search for Bitcoin Multibit Wallet to find their site.

Elected

- In addition to being quick and light, this wallet allows you to recover lost data using a passcode.
- Search for Bitcoin Elected Wallet to find their site.

After you get the wallet set up, take a few minutes clicking around. Things to look for:

- There will be a page that shows you how many bitcoins are currently in your wallet. Keep in mind that Bitcoins can be broken up into smaller pieces so that you may see a decimal with a lot of zeros after it. (Interesting note, 0.00000001 is one Satoshi, named after the pseudonymous creator of Bitcoin).
- There will be an area showing what your recent transactions are.
- There will be an area where you can create an address and a QR code (like the one I have above). You don't need the QR code if you don't want it, but if you run a business and you want to accept bitcoin, then all you'll need to do to accept payment is to show someone the QR code, let them take a picture of it, and they will be able to send you some money. You will also be able to create as many addresses as you like, so if you want to track where the money is coming from, you could have a separately labelled address from each one of your payees.
- There will be an area with a box for you to paste a code when you want to send money to someone or yourself on an exchange or different wallet.

There will be other options and features, but to start out with, these are the items that you should know about.

Getting Your First Bitcoins

Now that you have a wallet, you will, of course, want to test them out.

BITCOIN

There is the website that gives out small amounts of bitcoin for the purpose of getting people used to using them. The original version of this was run by the lead developer of Bitcoin, Gavin Andreson. That site has since closed, and this site operates by sending out one or two advertisements a month. You agree to receive those messages by requesting the bitcoins. Copy and paste your new bitcoin address and enter a phone number to which you can receive an SMS. They send out an SMS to be sure that people are not continuously coming back for more since it costs nothing to create a bitcoin address. They will also send out once or twice a month advertisement to support their operation. The amount they send it trivial: 0.0015 BTC (or 1.5 mBTC). However, they process almost immediately, and you can check to see that your address and wallet are working. It is also quite a feeling to get that portion of a bitcoin. (Non-disclaimer: I have no connection with this site and receive nothing if you use them. I simply think they are a good way to get your feet wet).

Congratulations! You have just entered the bitcoin economy.

To get your feet a little wetter, you can go panning for gold. There are some services and websites out there that will pay you in bitcoin to do things like go to certain websites, fill out online surveys, or watch sponsored videos. These are harmless, and you can earn a few extra bitcoins this way, but it is important to remember that these are businesses that get paid when people click on the links on their sites. They are essentially kicking back a portion of what they get paid to you. There is nothing illegal, or even immoral about this (you might like what you see and make a purchase!), but they are frequently flashy and may not be completely straightforward. All the ones that I have tried (particularly bitvisitor.com) have paid out as advertised. It is interesting to experiment with these, but even with the likely rise in the value of bitcoin, you won't become a millionaire doing this. So, unless you are an advertisement junkie, I would recommend you move on. If you would like to try, simply Google "free bitcoins" or something along those lines and you will find numerous sites.

Buying Bitcoin Hand-to-Hand

BITCOIN

Finally, this is going to be the real test of bitcoin. Can people easily trade them back and forth? If this can't happen, then there can't be a bitcoin economy because retailers won't be able to use it. If retailers can't use it, what earthly good is it? Fortunately, this is not a problem. IPhone is a bit of a holdout, but many smartphones have apps (mobile wallets) that will read QR codes and allow you to send bitcoin to whomever you want. You can also display a QR code of your address, or even carry a card in your wallet with your QR code to let people send bitcoin to you. Depending on what kind of wallet you have, you can then check to see if the bitcoins have been received.

A couple of things to note:

- When you set up your wallet, if you click around a bit, you will see an option to pay a fee to speed transactions. This money becomes available to a bitcoin miner as he/she/they process Bitcoin information. The miners doing the work of creating blocks of information keeps the system up to date and secure. The fee is an incentive to the miner to be sure to include your information in the next information block and therefore "verify" it. In the short term, miners are making most of their money by mining new coins (check the section on What Are Bitcoins for more information about this). In the long term, as it gets harder to find new coins, and as the economy increases, the fees will be an incentive for miners to keep creating more blocks and keep the economy going. Your wallet should be set to pay 0 fees as a default, but if you want, you can add a fee to priorities your transactions. You are under no obligation to pay a fee, and many organizations that process many small transactions (like the ones that pan for gold described above) produce enough fees to keep the miners happy.
- In clicking around your wallet, on the transactions page or linked to specific transactions, you will see a note about confirmations. When you make a transaction, that information is sent out into the network, and the network will send back a confirmation that there is no double entry for that bitcoin. It is smart to wait until you get several confirmations before walking away from someone who has

paid you. It is not very easy to scam someone hand-to-hand like this, and it is not very cost-effective for the criminal, but it can be done.

Where can you buy bitcoin like this?

- You may have a Bitcoin Meet up in your area.
- You can check out localbitcoins.com to find people near you who are interested in buying or selling.
- Some are trying to start up local street exchanges across the world. These are called Buttonwoods after the first street exchange established on Wall Street in 1792 under a buttonwood tree. See if there is one, or start one, in your area.
- See if you have any friends who would like to try bitcoins out. The more people who start using bitcoin, the larger and more successful it will come. So please tell two friends!

Some people ask if it is possible to buy physical bitcoins. The answer to this is both a yes and a no. Bitcoin, by its very nature, is a digital currency and has no physical form. However, there are a couple of ways that you can practically hold a bitcoin in your hands:

- ***Cascascius Coins***: These are the brainchild of Mike Caldwell. He mints physical coins and then embeds the private keys for the bitcoins inside them. You can get the private key by peeling a hologram from the coin which will then clearly show that the coin has been tampered with. Mike has gone out of his way to ensure that he can be trusted. These are a good investment strategy as in the years to come it may be that these coins are huge collector's items.
- ***Paper Wallets***: A paper wallet just means that rather than keeping the information for your bitcoin stored in a digital wallet, you print the key information off along with a private key and keep it safe in a safe, in a drawer, or in your mattress (if you like). This is highly recommended and cost effective

system for keeping your bitcoin safe. Keep in mind, though, that someone could steal them or if your house burns, they will go with the house and there will be no way to get them back. Really, no different than cash. Also, as with Casascius Coins, they will not be good for spending until you put them back into the computer.

There is software to make printing your paper wallets easier. Bitcoinpaperwallet.com is one of the best and includes a good tutorial about how to use them.

The bitcoins are not actually in the wallet, they are still on the web. In fact, the outside of the wallet will have a QR code that will allow you ship coins to the wallet any time you like.

The sealed part of the wallet will have the private key without which you cannot access the coins. Therefore, only put as many coins on the wallet as you want to be inaccessible. You will not be able to whip this thing out and take out a few coins to buy a cup of coffee. Rather, think of it as a piggy bank. To get the money, you have to smash it. It is possible to take out smaller amounts, but at this point, the security of the wallet is compromised, and it would be easier for someone to steal the coins. Better to have them all in or out.

People who use paper wallets are usually security conscious, and there are some ways for the nefarious in the world to hack your computer. Bitcoinpaperwallet.com gives a lot of good advice about how to print your wallets securely.

Some people have also asked about buying bitcoins on eBay. Yes, it is possible, but they will be far overpriced. So, selling on eBay might seem to be a better option given the extreme markup over market value you might see. But, as with anything that is too good to be true, this is too good to be true. As I will explain in the next section, selling bitcoin this way is just way too risky.

BITCOIN

How Not to Buy Bitcoin

In the next section, I am going to explain a couple of key points about buying from Bitcoin Exchanges. Before I do, let me give you a warning.

A short history lesson: When people first started setting up actual business based on bitcoin, they used all of the tools available to any merchant. They sold by credit card and PayPal. The problem with this business model was quickly spotted: bitcoin transactions are not reversible by anyone except the recipient of the money. Credit cards and PayPal have strong buyer protection policies that make it relatively easy for people to request a chargeback. So, nefarious individuals realized this and began making purchases of bitcoin and then sooner or later requesting a chargeback. And, since bitcoin is a non-physical product, sent by new and poorly understood technological means, the sellers were not able to contest this. Because of this, sellers stopped accepting credit cards and PayPal.

This was a big problem for the currency: How to move money between buyers and seller? Some business emerged that would credit you with bitcoin if you wired them money. Very often these businesses would give addresses in Albania, Poland, or Russia. The fact is that many of these did work and there are a lot of stories on the forums of people who bought bitcoins this way. But it took a lot of time and in the meantime the buyer just had to bite his or her fingernails wondering if they would get their bitcoins or kiss their investment goodbye.

I expect that as bitcoin becomes more acceptable and valuable, we are going to see a version of the Nigerian Prince scam. So the warning is this: we now have exchanges and other businesses that allow for moving money easily onto and off of exchanges. Never wire money for bitcoin. It was a short-lived, and well-forgotten, moment in the history of bitcoin.

There is no doubt in the fact that bitcoin trading is slowly taking the world of trading by storm. There is some hype, which says that bitcoin trading can be dangerous and difficult but honestly, it is a lot easier to get bitcoins, even easier than you think it is.

Here are some simple steps to buy bitcoin:

Find A Wallet

First of all, you have to find an e-wallet. It is basically a store or a provider that offers software from where bitcoins can be bought, stored, and traded. You can easily run it on your desktop, laptop, and even smartphones.

Sign Up

Next, you have to sign up with e-wallet. You will make an account that will let you store your bitcoins. The e-wallet trader will offer you a chance to convert your local currency into bitcoin. Therefore, the more local currency you have, the more bitcoins you can purchase.

Connect Your Bank Account

After signing up, the trader has to connect his bank account with his trading account. For this purpose, some verification steps are to be performed. Once the verifications are performed, then you can start purchasing bitcoins and get started.

Buying And Selling

Once you are done with your first purchase, your bank account will be debited and you will get the bitcoins. Selling is done in the same way purchasing is done. Keep in mind that the price of bitcoin changes time after time. The e-wallet you are working with will show you the current exchange rate. You should be aware of the rate before you buy.

Mining bitcoin

There is another way through which you can purchase bitcoins. This process is known as mining. Mining of bitcoins is similar to discovering gold from a mine. However, as mining gold is time consuming and a lot of effort is required, the same is the case with mining bitcoins. You have to solve a series of mathematical calculations that are designed by computer algorithms to win bitcoins for free. This is nearly impossible for a newbie. Traders have to open a series of padlocks in order to solve the mathematical calculations. In this procedure, you do not have to involve any kind of money to win bitcoins, as it is simply brainwork that lets you win bitcoins for free. The miners have to run software in order to win bitcoins with mining.

Bitcoin is a digital currency that is here to stay for a long time. Ever since it has been introduced, the trading of bitcoin has increased and it is on the rise even today. The value of bitcoin has also increased with its popularity. It is a new type of currency, which many traders are finding attractive just because of its earning potentials. At some places, bitcoins are even being used for purchasing commodities. Many online retailers are accepting bitcoin for the real time purchases too. There is a lot of scope for bitcoin in the coming era so buying bitcoins will not be a bad option.

By now you have probably heard of Bitcoin, but can you define it?

Most often it is described as a non-government digital currency. Bitcoin is also sometimes called a cybercurrency or, in a nod to its encrypted origins, a cryptocurrency. Those descriptions are accurate enough, but they miss the point. It's like describing the U.S. dollar as a green piece of paper with pictures on it.

I have my own ways of describing Bitcoin. I think of it as store credit without the store. A prepaid phone without the phone. Precious metal without the metal. Legal tender for no debts, public or private, unless the party to whom it is tendered wishes to accept it. An instrument backed by the full faith and credit only of its anonymous creators, in whom I therefore place no faith, and to whom I give no credit except for ingenuity.

I wouldn't touch a bitcoin with a 10-foot USB cable. But a fair number of people already have, and quite a few more soon may.

This is partly because entrepreneurs Cameron and Tyler Winklevoss, best known for their role in the origins of Facebook, are now seeking to use their technological savvy, and money, to bring Bitcoin into the mainstream.

BITCOIN

The Winklevosses hope to start an exchange-traded fund for bitcoins. An ETF would make Bitcoin more widely available to investors who lack the technological know-how to purchase the digital currency directly. As of April, the Winklevosses are said to have held around 1 percent of all existent bitcoins.

Created in 2009 by an anonymous cryptographer, Bitcoin operates on the premise that anything, even intangible bits of code, can have value so long as enough people decide to treat it as valuable. Bitcoins exist only as digital representations and are not pegged to any traditional currency.

According to the Bitcoin website, "Bitcoin is designed around the idea of a new form of money that uses cryptography to control its creation and transactions, rather than relying on central authorities." (1) New bitcoins are "mined" by users who solve computer algorithms to discover virtual coins. Bitcoins' purported creators have said that the ultimate supply of bitcoins will be capped at 21 million.

While Bitcoin promotes itself as "*a very secure and inexpensive way to handle payments*," (2) in reality few businesses have made the move to accept bitcoins. Of those that have, a sizable number operate in the black market.

Bitcoins are traded anonymously over the Internet, without any participation on the part of established financial institutions. As of 2012, sales of drugs and other black-market goods accounted for an estimated 20 percent of exchanges from bitcoins to U.S. dollars on the main Bitcoin exchange, called Mt. Gox. The Drug Enforcement Agency recently conducted its first-ever Bitcoin seizure, after reportedly tying a transaction on the anonymous Bitcoin-only marketplace Silk Road to the sale of prescription and illegal drugs.

Some Bitcoin users have also suggested that the currency can serve as a means to avoid taxes. That may be true, but only in the sense that bitcoins aid illegal tax evasion, not in the sense that they actually serve any role in genuine tax planning. Under federal tax law, no cash needs to change hands in order for a taxable transaction to occur. Barter and other non-cash exchanges are still fully taxable. There is no reason that transactions involving bitcoins would be treated differently.

Outside of the criminal element, Bitcoin's main devotees are speculators, who have no intention of using bitcoins to buy anything. These investors are convinced that the limited supply of bitcoins will force their value to follow a continual upward trajectory.

Bitcoin has indeed seen some significant spikes in value. But it has also experienced major losses, including an 80 percent decline over 24 hours in April. At the start of this month, bitcoins were down to around $90, from a high of $266 before the April crash. They were trading near $97 earlier this week, according to mtgox.com.

The Winklevosses would make Bitcoin investing easier by allowing smaller-scale investors to profit, or lose, as the case may be, without the hassle of actually buying and storing the electronic coins. Despite claims of security, Bitcoin storage has proved problematic. In 2011, an attack on the Mt. Gox exchange forced it to temporarily shut down and caused the price of bitcoins to briefly fall to nearly zero. Since Bitcoin transactions are all anonymous, there is little chance of tracking down the culprits if you suddenly find your electronic wallet empty. If the Winklevosses get regulatory approval, their ETF would help shield investors from the threat of individual theft. The ETF, however, would do nothing to address the problem of volatility caused by large-scale thefts elsewhere in the Bitcoin market.

While Bitcoin comes wrapped in a high-tech veneer, this newest of currencies has a surprising amount in common with one of the oldest currencies: gold. Bitcoin's own vocabulary, particularly the term **"mining**," highlights this connection, and intentionally so. The mining process is designed to be difficult as a control on supply, mimicking the extraction of more conventional resources from the ground. Far from providing a sense of security, however, this rhetoric ought to serve as a word of caution.

Gold is an investment of last resort. It has little intrinsic value. It does not generate interest. But because its supply is finite, it is seen as being more stable than forms of money that can be printed at will.

The problem with gold is that it doesn't do anything. Since gold coins have fallen out of use, most of the world's gold now sits in the vaults of central banks and other financial institutions. As a result, gold has little connection to the real economy. That can seem like a good thing when the real economy feels like a scary place to be. But as soon as other attractive investment options appear, gold loses its shine. That is what we have seen with the recent declines in gold prices.

In their push to bring Bitcoin to the mainstream, its promoters have accepted, and, in some cases sought out, increased regulation. Last month Mt. Gox registered itself as a money services business with the Treasury Department's Financial Crimes Enforcement Network. It has also increased customer verification measures. The changes came in response to a March directive from Financial Crimes Enforcement Network clarifying the application of its rules to virtual currencies. The Winklevosses' proposed ETF would bring a new level of accountability.

In the end, however, I expect that Bitcoin will fade back into the shadows of the black market. Those who want a regulated, secure currency that they can use for legitimate business transactions will pick from one of the many currencies already sponsored by a national government equipped with ample resources, a real-world economy and far more transparency and security than the Bitcoin world can offer.

After the Bitcoin bubble bursts, we won't even be able to use the leftover coins for jewelry.

WHAT MAKES BITCOIN SO VOLATILE?

Traders are always concerned about 'Bitcoin's volatility. It is important to know what makes the value of this particular digital currency highly unstable. Just like many other things, the value of 'Bitcoin' also depends upon the rules of demand and supply. If the demand for 'Bitcoin' increases, then the price will also increase. On the contrary side, the decrease in demand for the 'Bitcoin' will lead to decreased demand. In simple words, we can say that the price is determined by what amount the trading market is agreed to pay. If a large number of people wish to purchase 'Bitcoin's, then the price will rise. If more folks want to sell 'Bitcoin's, then the price will come down.

It is worth knowing that the value of **'Bitcoin'** can be volatile if compared to more established commodities and currencies. This fact can be credited to its comparatively small market size, which means that a lesser amount of money can shift the price of **'Bitcoin'** more prominently. This inconsistency will reduce naturally over the passage of time as the currency develops and the market size grows.

After being teased in late 2016, **'Bitcoin'** touched a new record high level in the first week of the current year. There could be several factors causing the **'Bitcoin'** to be volatile. Some of these are discussed here.

The Bad Press Factor

'Bitcoin' users are mostly scared by different news events including the statements by government officials and geopolitical events that 'Bitcoin' can be possibly regulated. It means the rate of 'Bitcoin' adoption is troubled by negative or bad press reports. Different bad news stories created fear in investors and prohibited them from investing in this digital currency. An example of bad headline news is the eminent utilization of 'Bitcoin' in processing drug transactions through Silk Road which came to an end with the FBI stoppage of the market in October 2013. This sort of stories produced panic among people and caused the 'Bitcoin' value to decrease greatly. On the other side, veterans in the trading industry saw such negative incidents as an evidence that the 'Bitcoin' industry is maturing. So the 'Bitcoin' started to gain its increased value soon after the effect of bad press vanished.

Fluctuations of the Perceived Value

Another great reason for 'Bitcoin' value to become volatile is the fluctuation of the 'Bitcoin's perceived value. You may know that this digital currency has properties akin to gold. This is ruled by a design decision by the makers of the core technology to restrict its production to a static amount, 21 million BTC. Due to this factor, investors may allocate less or more assets in into 'Bitcoin'.

News about Security Breaches

Various news agencies and digital media play an important role in building a negative or positive public concept. If you see something being advertised advantageously, you are likely to go for that without paying much attention to negative sides. There has been news about 'Bitcoin' security breaches and it really made the investors think twice before investing their hard earned money in 'Bitcoin' trading. They become too susceptible about choosing any specific 'Bitcoin' investment platform. 'Bitcoin' may become volatile when 'Bitcoin' community uncovers security susceptibilities in an effort to create a great open source response in form of security fixes. Such security concerns give birth to several open-source software such as Linux. Therefore, it is advisable that 'Bitcoin' developers should expose security vulnerabilities to the general public in order to make strong solutions.

The latest 'OpenSSL' weaknesses attacked by 'Heartbleed' bug and reported by Neel Mehta (a member of Google's security team) on April 1, 2014, appear to had some descending effect on the value of 'Bitcoin'. According to some reports, the 'Bitcoin' value decreased up to 10% in the ensuing month as compared to the U.S. Dollar.

Small option value for holders of large 'Bitcoin' Proportions

The volatility of 'Bitcoin' also depends upon 'Bitcoin' holders having large proportions of this digital currency. It is not clear for 'Bitcoin' investors (with current holdings over $10M) that how they would settle a position that expands into a fiat position without moving the market severely. So 'Bitcoin' has not touched the bulk market adoption rates that would be important to give option value to large 'Bitcoin' holders.

Effects of Mt Gox

The recent high-profile damages at 'Mt Gox' are another great reason for the 'Bitcoin' volatility. All these losses and the resultant news about heavy losses had a dual effect on instability. You may not know that this reduced the general float of 'Bitcoin' by almost 5%. This also created a potential lift on the residual 'Bitcoin' value due to the reason of increased scarcity. Nevertheless, superseding this lift was the negative outcome of the news series that followed. Particularly, many other 'Bitcoin' gateways saw the large failure at Mt Gox as an optimistic thing for the long-term prospects of the 'Bitcoin'.

BITCOIN VALUE

What is the actual value of BitCoins? To understand the BitCoin value, we need to first understand the true meaning of the word "*value*" - since everyone considers the value of an item differently. The "*value*" of an item relates directly to its perceived benefits and usefulness to the individual holding the item. So in other words, an item's "*value*" is rather subjective.

Do not make the mistake of confusing an item's value and its price. The price of an item only refers to how much money you'll need to give in order to acquire said item - but that does not relate to its value. For example, a new car may seem valuable to you, but it may not mean anything to a billionaire who already owns one hundred cars.

So like any other item, the BitCoin value is determined by its usefulness - such as its advantages over fiat currencies and its growing acceptance as a legitimate form of "*legal tender*". Let's have a look at three main features that determine the value of BitCoins.

The BitCoin Value To The Science and Technology Community

One of the biggest problems in creating an acceptable worldwide digital currency was ensuring proper record keeping of transactions by all parties involved. This problem was solved by Satoshi Nakamoto's clever solution called the BitCoin Block Chain.

The Block chain is a shared public ledger, and is maintained by the peer-to-peer nodes that populate the entire Bitcoin network. It is a world-wide, self-organizing, time-based, public consensus database that anyone can view.

When you download and install a BitCoin wallet onto your computer or mobile device, you are instantly connected to this peer-to-peer network. Every transaction that you perform is placed within the record. No duplicate entries are allowed - even if you were to copy the contents of an entire BitCoin wallet onto another computer or mobile device.

Bitcoin transactions are digitally signed with very complex hash entries to ensure that no one tries to modify the transactions. This makes BitCoin transactions very secure.

The peer-to-peer (decentralized) nature of the BitCoin network ensures that no one person, cooperation or government can control the BlockChain data. This great feature makes BitCoins "censorship resistant". No government can "ban BitCoins" as you cannot ban something that you have absolutely no control of.

You do not require the approval of anyone to use BitCoins and this ensures that BitCoins are indeed here to stay - much to the annoyance of the naysayers.

BitCoin Value and Trust

There once was a time when you could have "trusted" your life savings with a bank. You also could have "trusted" your government to give you your pension when you retire. Those days are gone. Banks and governments have proven beyond the shadow of a doubt that they are completely incapable of maintaining the trust of citizens. This is one of the main reasons why BitCoins are growing in popularity.

BITCOIN

With BitCoins, you never have to worry about placing any trust in a central authority - since no one person, bank or government can centralize BitCoins. The problem of "*placing trust*" is completely eradicated from the system.

The BitCoin protocol was designed to function on its own - viewed by everyone, but manipulated by no one. You can only control the amount of BitCoins that you have in your wallet - nothing more.

The BitCoin protocol ushers in a new age in currency exchange - where everyone has direct control over their own personal finances - without having it arbitrarily taken away or misused by any central authority.

BitCoin Value and Security

Bitcoins transactions are secure because they utilize the public/private key pair system. Bitcoin addresses are public keys that are created by corresponding private keys. The private keys are stored within a user's wallet.

CHAPTER 2: BITCOIN HISTORY

BITCOIN HISTORY

When BitCoins were first released in early 2009, there was no price associated with BitCoins since there were no existing currencies that could be directly exchanged for them. Some early adopters began getting involved in BitCoins since they saw its potential as an alternative medium of exchange.

Bitcoin Price

The BitCoin community grew and the BitCoin price in January 2011 was at $0.30. Its value was mainly based against the U.S dollar, and it still is (as of this writing). After many ups and downs, the BitCoin price landed at around $4.25 by the end of 2011.

Bitcoins (like paper currency) will always go through trends of volatility. Unlike paper currency, however, bitcoins have two advantages:

1. Only a limited amount of BitCoins will ever be on the World BitCoin Exchange (Block Chain). This safety net ensures that BitCoin traders will never run into a case of "runaway inflation". Multiple countries around the world are currently suffering from financial mismanagement of their paper currencies and citizens are turning to alternative currencies - like BitCoins.
2. BitCoin trading is decentralised - all computers from around the world (including mobile devices) can connect to the exchange network. This decentralised nature ensures that no one individual, corporation, government or bank can have the ability to easily manipulate the BitCoin price. But that does not stop them from trying.

BitCoin Price - Wild Market Speculators

In 2013, the popularity of BitCoins grew even further. Wild speculators began jumping in and out of the market. From January to April, the BitCoin price shot up from $13.25 to $266.00. A price correction kicked in and pulled the price down to $50.00 a week later.

The United States Senate needed to have a "hearing" about BitCoins that year (because when you cannot control something that is not meant to be controlled by any government, having a so-called "hearing" is important - note the sarcasm).

The BitCoin price peaked at around $1,240.00, but finally settled down to $800.00 by the end of 2013. It was pretty obvious that wild speculators were trying to treat BitCoins with the same wild abandon as in the "paper currency stock markets."

The year of 2014 was the year of "market correction" where the price trend went down until the BitCoin price was about $325.00. This year was also very important because it was the year of the "BitCoin Venture Capitalists". Over $300 million dollars of venture capital investments were used to expand and enhance the Bitcoin network infrastructure.

This expanded and enhanced infrastructure is what allows people from anywhere in the world to easily get a BitCoin wallet and begin trading in BitCoins - without having to be a "technology wizard".

BitCoin Price - Stable Investing and Beyond

Venture Capitalists are adding more investment capital into the BitCoin infrastructure and BitCoins are now recognised as a true and viable alternative currency in many countries around the world. More and more online companies are accepting BitCoins as a form of payment.

The worldwide acceptance of BitCoins is very important to the stability of the BitCoin price. If you have not invested in BitCoins as yet, then there is no better time than now to do so. The BitCoin currency has indeed proven itself to be a viable alternative medium of exchange.

We will soon be upon the BitCoin Halving Event. There is allot of speculation going around about the significance of this event and how it affects the price of BitCoins. This article will explain what the BitCoin halving event is all about and how it affects the BitCoin community.

BitCoin Halving - Keeping The Limit

There is a limit to the maximum amount of BitCoins that can ever be created. The BitCoin protocol dictates that BitCoins are generated in blocks. It also dictates that the number of BitCoins generated per block is set to decrease geometrically (by 50%) every 210,000 blocks.

What does this mean with regards to BitCoin generation? Approximately six blocks are generated on average within an hour, and halving takes place once every 210,000 blocks. This means that there will be a halving event approximately every four years.

BitCoin Halving and BitCoin Mining

People who partake in performing BitCoin computations (mining) are rewarded with BitCoins. So how does this event affect people who mine BitCoins? The reward for mining BitCoins will be effectively cut in half. So if each miner is rewarded with 25 Bitcoins for solving a block, after the halving event, he will be rewarded with 12.5 BitCoins per block.

The BitCoin protocol dictates that a total amount of 21 million BitCoins will ever be created. This goal is expected to be achieved by the year 2140. The BitCoin halving event is the method that is used to ensure that this goal (and this limit) is achieved.

Why BitCoin Halving Is Necessary

The following is a quote from Vitalik But from BitCoin Magazine:

"The main reason why this is done is to keep inflation under control. One of the major faults of traditional, "fiat", currencies controlled by central banks is that the banks can print as much of the currency as they want, and if they print too much, the laws of supply and demand ensure that the value of the currency starts dropping quickly.

Bitcoin, on the other hand, is intended to simulate a commodity, like gold. There is only a limited amount of gold in the world, and with every gramme of gold that is mined, the gold that remains becomes harder and harder to extract. As a result of this limited supply, gold has maintained its value as an international medium of exchange and store of value for over six thousand years, and the hope is that Bitcoin will do the same."

As you can see from the above-mentioned quote, the importance of maintaining a limited supply of BitCoins is paramount in maintaining its value as a viable alternative to fiat currency. Without the BitCoin halving event taking place, then we might as well just continue using wasteful paper currency.

BitCoin Halving and The BitCoin Community

So this brings us to the inevitable questions that are being asked around the world:

1. How does this event affect the BitCoin community?
2. How will this affect the BitCoin price?

When it comes to the question of price, there are only two scenarios that are being forecasted: the price will dramatically rise, or the price will stay the same. At this point, there is little to no chance of any dramatic price drop, since BitCoins are following the same economic rules of demand and supply.

This same debate took place before the Bitcoin halving event back in 2012. The result was that nothing happened to the price. But keep in mind that the BitCoin community in 2012 was much smaller than it is today. When it comes to commodities, it's a known fact that past trends cannot accurately predict future trends.

Previous trends have shown that the BitCoin price tends to be more affected by external economic forces, rather than by the halving event. The BitCoin halving event takes place approximately every four years. Whether or not this event would play a role in drastic price changes, remains to be seen

Around 2009 a new concept of currency was introduced. The concept seemed a little vague about the usage of this currency, but two years later, Bitcoins has emerged as a fast catching trend. Proclaimed as a decentralised digital currency, more people and business have started using Bitcoins. Though the currency is still in its experimental stage regular updating and frequent tweaking is done to improve it in every way possible. Unlike other banking networks Bitcoins are not controlled by anyone. The network has a set of protocols protected by cryptography. It's a new payment system which has no central authority other than the cryptography (open source software working with the laws of mathematics) which handles the creation and transaction, making it impossible to cheat around the system. The Bitcoins share a public ledger (block chain ledger) where every transaction is recorded making it a prominent triple entry bookkeeping system and a transparent recorder. Using the peer to peer system and a cryptographic key, transactions are processed between clients. As the key cannot be deciphered it's a more safe form of internet cash than performing transactions with credit and debit cards.

As with every new emerging trend, the Bitcoins have advantages and disadvantages. But if the obstacles are removed, it might help re-imaging of International finance. The advantages of Bitcoins are

The users have total control over the money, they can send and receive any amount of payments at time of the day. As these transactions are not performed by banks or organizations but between individuals it's easy as sending a file.

The transactions require no or very less money compared to other online money transfers which stick up a hefty fee, the only service in Bitcoins is done by the miners to facilitate the transaction recording on the block and that doesn't cost much.

This is the most secure and irreversible form of cash transactions where no personal information is traded. Most people will opt for this method as it removes major hassles involved in other transactions.

Large markets and small businesses have widely accepted it as it helps in quicker and reliable money transfers with very little administration cost.

When other currencies are affected by price fluctuations, the same cannot be said for Bitcoins.

The disadvantages of Bitcoins are listed below though they can be turned around. The new rules and updates are being constantly worked on by various trusted parties to help shape this up.

There is no guarantee and no purchasing power provided yet.

The Bitcoin price has yet to stabilise, which can only happen when the number of users and businesses using bitcoins increase.

Client programs used as wallets cannot guarantee or provide insurance on the Bitcoins.

The currency has yet to mature and get a better hold on the market.

The challenges faced by Bitcoins can be easily deterred. But the currency needs a stronger presence and better guarantees on the safety before it can be accepted widely by the public as the easiest form of online currency. The concept at present is a successful online currency venture which is on an adventurous trail. It has yet to be legalised and changed from an experimental currency. Though the future of Bitcoins is nothing but speculation, it has a positive response from all its users and might just be the next big thing.

BITCOIN FUTURE TRENDS

Bitcoin brokers are increasingly becoming an important aspect when it comes to trading bitcoin. When you get the right broker, you will be on your way to getting value for your money as they are often created at a predictable and decreasing rate. Over time the numbers of bitcoins created every year are often halved automatically until their issuance halts completely to 21 million of those in existence. When it gets to this point, miners are supported exclusively by small transaction fees.

Becoming a major payment system

The system can process several transactions every second. Nevertheless, the system is not entirely ready to scale up to the level of credit card networks. Work is underway to raise the current limitations, besides the future requirements being well known. Since its inception, every aspect of the system has been on a continuous trend of maturation, specialisation and optimisation. And this process is expected to stay the same way for some years to come. Furthermore, as the traffic grows, more users of the system are expected to use lightweight clients.

In the event of loss

If a user loses his/her wallet, money is often removed from circulation. Nevertheless, bitcoins remain in the chain just like others. But lost bitcoins often remain dormant indefinitely because nobody can find the private key(s) that would enable them to be used again. Based on the principle of demand and supply, when the market has fewer, the demand for those which are available will be high, which translates to increased value or prices of the ones which are available in the market.

Bitcoins and illegal activities

Concerns are often raised that the system can be used to facilitate illegal activities. However, these features exist with wire and cash transfers which are well established and widely used. Usage will be subjected to the same regulations that have been established within existing financial systems. The system is unlikely to prevent criminal investigations being conducted. It is not uncommon for important breakthroughs to be seen as being controversial long before their merits are well understood.

Regulation

It is possible for the use of bitcoins to be regulated the same way other instruments are regulated. Just like money, they can be utilised for a variety of purposes including both legitimate and illegitimate based on the laws within a particular jurisdiction. Therefore, they are not different from other tools or resources. Nonetheless, they can be subjected to diverse regulations in every country under consideration.

CHAPTER 3: BITCOIN TRADING

Bitcoins are the newest form of digital currency being used by many traders and investors. Any exchange market can trade bitcoins, but it's a risky shot, as you can lose your hard earned money. One should be quite cautious before proceeding.

A bitcoin is the same as currency, though it is digital in form. You can save it, invest it and spend it. Crypto-currency once circulated the market and gave rise to the Bitcoin. This started in 2009 by an anonymous person with a nickname of Satoshi Nakamoto. The bitcoin has gained popularity during this year as its rate jumped from $2 to $266. This happened during the months of February and April. A process known as mining is said to generate a Bitcoin using powerful computer algorithms called blocks. Once a block has been decrypted, you earn about 50 Bitcoins. Usually, solving a single problem takes a lot of time, maybe a year or so. If you cannot do so, then there is another medium to get these Bitcoins; that is you simply buy them.

When you buy a Bitcoin, you exchange your physical money and get the digital currency in the form of a Bitcoin. It is very simple, if you want to exchange currency, you have to pay for it to get that currency. Same is the case with the Bitcoins. You pay the current rate of Bitcoin. Let's suppose it is $200 so you pay $200 and get one Bitcoin. It's a type of commodity. Most of the exchanges operating in the market make a lot of money by moving the currency in the market. They get US dollars by giving these Bitcoins and get rich instantly. But the thing is that as it seems easy to make money by converting the Bitcoins into Dollars, these exchanges lose their money quite easily too.

There are several ways of becoming players in the Bitcoin market. The simplest way is to buy a dedicated computer and install some Bitcoins mining software and start decrypting the blocks. This process is said to be the easiest possible way, but it's slow.

If you want to make money faster, then you have to form a team. You should organise a Bitcoin pool comprising of four to five members. Then you can form a mining pool and can decrypt the blocks faster than an individual can do. You would end up decrypting several blocks simultaneously.

The quickest way to make money through Bitcoins is that you should go straight to the markets. Go for the reputable and reliable Bitcoins exchanges operating in the market. You first of all have to register yourself. Sign up and make an account and then you must respond to the confirmations accordingly. This will keep you up to date on all the working stocks of the Bitcoins. You can trade bitcoins at any online trading platform. Some companies have even started accepting payments in bitcoins.

Bitcoin is a revolutionary kind of currency that was introduced in 2009! It functions by enabling transactions to go through without the need for the middle man. Therefore no banks are required.

You also get the benefit of no transaction fees and no need giving out your real name. With such flexibility bitcoin has become widely accepted by both consumers and merchants. It also can be used to purchase web hosting services, foods online, and just about any service you can think of online.

Bitcoin has impacted much on the currency arena. It can be easily utilized to purchase merchandise anonymously. It also provides the benefits of easy and cheap international payments and is not subjected or limited to any country or regulation.

Some people see Bitcoin as a vehicle for investments and buy Bitcoin by trusting that they will increase in value.

To get Bitcoins, you can purchase on an Exchange marketplace that allows people buy or sell them, utilizing other various currencies.

The transferring of Bitcoins is easily done by forwarding Bitcoins to one another person utilizing mobile apps or their PCs online. It's just like sending cash digitally.

With Bitcoins you have a currency value that can be stored in what's called a "digital wallet," which subsists either within the cloud or on a computer. This digital wallet is like a virtual bank account that lets account holders within it send or receive Bitcoins, purchase goods and services or store them.

Although most bank accounts are insured by the FDIC, Bitcoin wallets are not, yet they are safe, secure and have payment flexibility benefits.

Unlike the US dollar, gold, silver, or some other precious metals, Bitcoins are scarce and this scarcity is algorithmic.

In terms of international remittance Bitcoin is a winner. There is no worry about fraud or security. At some money exchange businesses for instance, migrant workers could utilize Bitcoin to send payments from one nation to another via email.

On the 27th of June in 2014, the US Government was scheduled to auction off about 30,000 BTC that was confiscated from the shutdown of Silk Road, an online black market operation. At that time, the value of Bitcoins was 633.84 dollars. Today, one Bitcoin is worth about $655.48 US dollars around the time that this article was written.

If you take a good look at some the local merchants downtown, the inner cities or online, you will see the Bitcoin logo acceptance in the window or on the door.

Bitcoin is still maturing and is making a tremendous progression towards being one of the most sensible currencies ever created.

BITCOIN IMPACT ON CURRENCY

Bitcoin is a revolutionary kind of currency that was introduced in 2009! It functions by enabling transactions to go through without the need for the middle man. Therefore no banks are required.

You also get the benefit of no transaction fees and no need giving out your real name. With such flexibility, bitcoin has become widely accepted by both consumers and merchants. It also can be used to purchase web hosting services, foods online, and just about any service, you can think of online.

Bitcoin has impacted much on the currency arena. It can be easily utilised to purchase merchandise anonymously. It also provides the benefits of easy and cheap international payments and is not subjected or limited to any country or regulation.

BITCOIN

Some people see Bitcoin as a vehicle for investments and buy Bitcoin by trusting that they will increase in value.

To get Bitcoins, you can purchase on an Exchange marketplace that allows people buy or sell them, utilising other various currencies.

The transferring of Bitcoins is easily done by forwarding Bitcoins to one another person utilising mobile apps or their PCs online. It's just like sending cash digitally.

With Bitcoins, you have a currency value that can be stored in what's called a "***digital wallet***," which subsists either within the cloud or on a computer. This digital wallet is like a virtual bank account that lets account holders within it send or receive Bitcoins, purchase goods and services or store them.

Although most bank accounts are insured by the FDIC, Bitcoin wallets are not, yet they are safe, secure and have payment flexibility benefits.

Unlike the US dollar, gold, silver, or some other precious metals, Bitcoins are scarce, and this scarcity is algorithmic.

Regarding international remittance, Bitcoin is a winner. There is no worry about fraud or security. At some money exchange businesses, for instance, migrant workers could utilise Bitcoin to send payments from one nation to another via email.

On the 27th of June in 2014, the US Government was scheduled to auction off about 30,000 BTC that was confiscated from the shutdown of Silk Road, an online black market operation. At that time, the value of Bitcoins was 633.84 dollars.

If you take a good look at some the local merchants downtown, the inner cities or online, you will see the Bitcoin logo acceptance in the window or on the door.

Bitcoin is still maturing and is making a tremendous progression towards being one of the most sensible currencies ever created.

CHAPTER 4: BITCOIN IN NUTSHELL

BITCOIN REALITY

Is Bitcoin real money? Not according to Alan Greenspan, who recently described the entire phenomenon as a '*bubble*'. The People's Bank of China concurred that it isn't a currency with '**real meaning**' and backed that up by banning financial companies from making Bitcoin transactions.

Of course, this raises some questions, such as what is the meaning of '*real meaning*'? Why is Bitcoin a bubble, but not the housing market in 2006? And what exactly is a Bitcoin anyway? The main feature of Bitcoin, which distinguishes it from conventional currencies such as the yuan or the dollar, is that it is produced and maintained by a network of computers, rather than by a central bank. The other main difference is that you can't use it to buy much, and you certainly can't pay your taxes with it.

In other respects, though, Bitcoin is not so different from conventional currencies. Bitcoin is a 'virtual' currency, in the sense that it only exists as a string of digital information that you can download to a '**digital wallet**'. But the British pound or US dollar is also best described as virtual currencies. As outlined in a recent paper from the Bank of England, the vast majority of money is created by private banks and ushered into existence by pressing a button on a keyboard. The central bank plays a relatively small role in the money supply process, primarily by setting its interest rates.

The difference between Bitcoins and state-backed currencies is, therefore, smaller than appearances suggest. Both are virtual currencies that run on computer networks. Mobile phones, for example, are increasingly used as a kind of electronic wallet. The primary advantage of Bitcoin, though, is that it was designed from the outset to work this way.

Block chain

For example, while we are all used to making purchases over the internet, the process is clunky and involves some middlemen, such as credit card companies, who charge transaction fees. These middlemen are necessary to make sure that the money has left your account and is deposited in the store's account. Unfortunately, the process is not completely secure, which is why most credit card fees go to paying for fraud.

The main challenge of digital transactions is how to avoid things like double spending. One reason the music industry is in so much trouble, for example, is that it is possible to send a digital copy of a song to somebody else while keeping your copy. If this were to happen with money, it would be great for a while, but would soon lead to chaos, since you could spend your paycheck as many times as you wanted (I have tried this, and it doesn't work).

The main innovation of Bitcoin is that transactions are recorded on a secure, anonymous, public ledger, known as a block chain, which is maintained by a network of computers that make such shenanigans impossible. Unlike digital music, you can't share your Bitcoins with a friend or eat out of them multiple times. And without middlemen, transactions are faster, cheaper, and more secure.

Maintaining the block chain requires a lot of number crunching. The task is carried out by a network of computers that communicate through a shared protocol and is currently rewarded by the granting of Bitcoins. Just as traditional currencies used to rely on their backing on supplies of gold, today people 'mine' for digital gold. According to some estimates, the electricity used to mine Bitcoins would power some three million homes.

The issuing of new coins will end when the total number reaches 21 million, which should happen sometime around 2140. After that, mining will only be rewarded by a regular transaction fee. One of the attractions of Bitcoin for many people is that its value can't be inflated away by turning on the digital printing press, as governments are wont to do.

BITCOIN

Real meaning

So why would Bitcoin not have 'real meaning'? According to Greenspan, the main problem seems to be that it is not produced in the normal way through a central authority. "I do not understand where the backing of Bitcoin is coming from," he has said. *"There is no fundamental issue of capabilities of repaying it in anything which is universally acceptable, which is either the intrinsic value of the currency or the credit or trust of the individual who is issuing the money, whether it's a government or an individual."*

But why should only a government or monarch be able to back a currency? Bitcoin is backed by something equally significant, if more distributed and amorphous: its network of users. The only thing that makes the US dollar 'real' is that it is accepted by the government as an official means of payment. The main thing that has dissuaded potential Bitcoin users is the currency's volatility, and its connection with anonymous transactions. But volatility may come down as the user pool grows larger and more diverse, and as new tools for insurance and currency, hedging becomes available. And associations with things like crime or drug running never put people on the hundred-dollar bill.

In any case, the most disruptive feature of Bitcoin is not its status as a potential rival for mainstream currencies, but the technical innovation of the block chain, which allows for anonymous and secure transactions over the internet. The potential for such a system was foreseen by **Milton Friedman**, who said in 1999: "I think that the internet is going to be one of the major forces for reducing the role of government.

"And the one thing that's missing, but that will soon be developed, is a reliable e-cash, a method whereby on the Internet you can transfer funds from A to B, without A knowing B or B knowing A.

The way in which I can take a 20 dollar bill and hand it over to you, and there's no record of where it came from." No wonder central banks don't think the Bitcoin is real.

CHAPTER 5: BITCOIN WALLET

In a relatively short space of time, BitCoins have earned its place as a viable alternative to paper (fiat) currency.

With that said, it is essential for you to know what BitCoin wallets are and how to store your BitCoins in your wallet safely. You will need to treat your BitCoin wallet in the same way that you treat your physical wallet in your pocket. You would not leave your wallet on some random table for anyone to pick up, now would you?

You can create your BitCoin wallet either offline or online. The method that you use is directly dependent on your security needs.

Having a BitCoin Wallet Online.

With an online BitCoin wallet, you can easily perform transactions in any location where you have internet access and on any desktop or mobile device. This gives you the freedom, for example, of moving to another country with well over $10,000 worth of BitCoins.

The security measures in place for keeping your Bitcoins online are getting better every day. But like everything else in life - nothing is perfect. If the website where you store your Bitcoins does not have a high amount of security, there's a good chance that the website could get hacked. If this happens, some or even all of your Bitcoins can be stolen - and there are no ways to automatically retrieve Bitcoins once they are transferred to another account.

There are ways of increasing the security of your online wallet such as enabling two-factor authentication (available on all reputable online wallets), where you can enter your password and then receive a text message on your mobile phone with a second code.

Besides using two-factor authentication, you should also use a lengthy password (mixed with letters, numbers and symbols) and make sure to back up your wallet in an offline location.

Nothing is completely impervious to persistent hackers, but using these strategies will give hackers a really hard time - thereby forcing them to move to easier targets.

Here is a list of popular online Bitcoin wallets:

- Bitfinex
- CoinBase
- Xapo

Having a BitCoin Wallet Offline.

If you are worried about your BitCoins being stolen from your online wallet, then your best alternative is to download an offline wallet and store your BitCoins on your desktop computer.

Here's a list of popular desktop BitCoin wallets for both Windows and Mac computers:

- BitCoin Core
- MultiBit HD
- Electrum
- mSIGNA
- Copay
- Bither
- BitGo
- Green Address

If you are not very tech savvy when it comes to BitCoins, then it is recommended that you should use one of the simpler Bitcoin wallets.

BITCOIN

An offline BitCoin wallet needs to do the following:

1. Connect to the BitCoin network (Block Chain) with a high amount of security.
2. Securely perform outgoing Bitcoin transactions.
3. Securely perform incoming BitCoin transactions.
4. Store your BitCoin wallet data on your computer.
5. Backup your BitCoin wallet data to a remote location (like your Drop Box account for example).

Bitcoin wallets would have different additional features, but the ones mentioned above are the most important. Take your time and see which one of these wallets would be right for you.

Bitcoins can be stored in various ways, either as digital assets or as physical assets, either online or offline. One way in which you can store BitCoins in a physical format is by creating a BitCoin paper wallet. Creating a BitCoin paper wallet is also known as placing your BitCoins in "**Cold Storage**".

Bitcoins, being a digital currency, is, of course, subject to the possibility of attacks from hackers who, motivated by greed, would like nothing better than to steal your assets instead of acquiring their own. This is exactly why BitCoins were created with multiple options for storage.

Placing your BitCoins in "**Cold Storage**" is a good way to ensure the security and safety of your BitCoins, but there are factors that you would need to consider when using this method.

How to Create A Bitcoin Paper Wallet

In its simplest terms, a BitCoin paper wallet is simply the digital codes of your BitCoin data, printed directly onto a sheet of paper. The paper wallet contains copies of the public and the private keys that are used to access your BitCoin data.

BITCOIN

It goes without saying that it is very important to hide your printed data in a safe place (like a safety deposit box for example). If an unauthorised person gets access to your paper wallet (and they know how to use it), then your BitCoins are gone. A

Another factor to keep in mind is that paper and ink degrade over time, so make sure that this document is in a safe and dry place. Don't forget to have a look at it every once in a while and print out another one if needed.

To perform a transaction from your paper wallet, all you'll need to do is scan the QR Codes (also printed on your paper wallet) and add the data to your software wallet.

Creating a BitCoin paper wallet is very simple. Follow the steps below to create your wallet:

1. Go to the following website: http://www.bitaddress.org/
2. Move your mouse cursor around the screen for about 30 seconds or randomly enter characters in the box provided. This adds extra random data to your keys - making it even more secure.
3. Once the process is complete, a new page will automatically open. Your public and private keys will be displayed with their respective QR codes.
4. Next, click on the "**Paper Wallet**" tab.
5. Specify the number of BitCoin addresses that you would like to generate. Modify other settings as needed.
6. Click on the "**Generate**" button.
7. Once the wallets are generated, click on the "**Print**" button to print out your BitCoin paper wallets. Make sure to use high-quality paper - keeping in mind the important factors of proper storage that were mentioned above.

Bitcoin itself is something called a "***cryptocurrency***," which means that it is 100% digital and is protected and maintained by a very advanced set of military grade public key algorithms that require solving complex mathematical equations.

A Currency Powered By an Algorithm

The computer network that solves these equations is peer-to-peer in nature, meaning that it is a collection of interconnected computers from all over the world. There is a very large file that some digital wallets will require you to download called the block chain, which is the total of every Bitcoin transaction that has ever occurred. One of the implications of the block chain as part of the Bitcoin algorithm is that every single transaction is recorded permanently as a matter of public record, meaning that Bitcoin is not anonymous and can be used to identify the people behind certain transactions.

Purchasing and Paying In Bitcoins

If you want to own or purchase bitcoins, then the first step that you need to take is to download the free digital wallet software to either your computer or your smartphone. Many people choose to make use of the smartphone version of the digital wallet because it allows them to carry their bitcoins with them as well as make purchases in person by paying with bitcoins. The way that you can pay using bitcoins in person instead of just on the internet is that the merchant can use their smartphone to generate an invoice that has a QR code, which is a square shaped black and white box that you can capture with your smartphone to complete the transaction.

Protect and Secure Your Digital Wallet

Because the new Bitcoin cryptocurrency is entirely digital, it is important to be extremely cautious when it comes to protecting your digital wallet to make sure that your money is not compromised in any way. It is crucial to keep your private password safe so that you never forget it and so nobody else has access to it, and it is also a bad idea to ever post your Bitcoin address on the internet. By learning more about Bitcoin and how to use the digital wallet software you can decide whether you want to convert some of your money into Bitcoins to take advantage of the newly decentralised cryptocurrency.

CHAPTER 6: BITCOIN EXCHANGE RATE

If you are an investor or early adopter of the Bitcoin digital currency then an important metric that you will want to monitor is the Bitcoin exchange rate as it relates to US dollars as denominated by the symbol BTC. It is realistic to say that Bitcoins are still in their early adopter phase of technology even though an increasing number of stores and ATMs accept the digital currency, and anyone who has some of their money denominated in Bitcoins should monitor the exchange rate on a regular basis to see what their investment constitutes in a dollar equivalent.

Trading The Bitcoin Exchange Rate

There are some advanced traders and investors who are participating in the Bitcoin digital marketplace that are not buying the digital currency to buy and hold it over a long period of time, but instead are trading the Bitcoin exchange rate up and down the same way that you would trade the price of a major currency pair. It is also important to understand the differences between denominating your money in Bitcoins and denominating it in a regular first world currency such as the dollar, pound, or euro.

There is a lot of safety and financial stability in the major world currencies that exists and will persist, yet there are a number of revolutionary benefits associated with Bitcoin that are seen as very promising even though it is still a bit risky. One of the major differences is that all Bitcoins exist in digital form as a piece of software code instead of being a physical asset that you can touch with your hands like cash or gold. This means that all of your Bitcoin holdings are contained in your digital wallet which is a software program that can run on your desktop computer, laptop, or mobile phone.

The Price Volatility Associated With Bitcoins

One of the characteristics about investing or trading in Bitcoins that many individuals see as a risky disadvantage is that the price of Bitcoins is extremely volatile and it has been known to move over $100 in just several days. This is not a positive feature if you are someone who is trying to passively invest in Bitcoins by buying and holding them in order to try and see your asset value increase over time. While Bitcoin is still in its experimental phases there are more and more people using the new digital currency every day, and by learning about how the Bitcoin exchange rate performs you can decide if you are ready to jump on the Bitcoin bandwagon

For those people who are looking to buy real Bitcoins one of the most popular options is to use a company called a Bitcoin exchange where you are allowed to trade your currency such as euros, pound, or dollars into Bitcoins. It is important for individual investors to understand some of the risks associated with Bitcoins and to know that transacting with a Bitcoin exchange is not always necessarily safe as there have been several Bitcoin exchange companies that have been shut down due to fraudulent behaviour.

Look For Online Reviews Before Buying

There are a small number of Bitcoin exchanges today that have established themselves as industry leaders, and these companies will have a large number of positive reviews on the internet. Just as you might do if you were considering making any other sort of purchase on the internet, you should take the time to check the reviews and see what other people have to say about their experiences working with that company. Stay away from exchanges that have a large number of negative reviews and a small number of positive reviews.

Independent Digital Wallet Or Bitcoin Exchange Account?

It is important to understand the difference between having your digital wallet software that you are running on your computer or mobile phone where your Bitcoins are stored and set up an account at a Bitcoin exchange company where your Bitcoins will be stored. The primary difference between these two is that you alone will have complete 100% control over your digital wallet if it is stored on your device, and you will have less control if you store your Bitcoins in an account at a Bitcoin exchange company. The ideal situation would be to have your Bitcoins in your digital wallet since you become more dependent on the exchange company since they are going to be the ones who control your account.

When Is The Right Time To Buy?

You will notice if you check the prices offered by different Bitcoin exchanges that the prices not only fluctuate on a daily basis, but some Bitcoin exchanges will offer better and more affordable prices than some of the other ones do. It is up to you whether you want to buy at the current market price or wait for a better price and whether you want to shop around at the different exchanges to try and find the best purchase price possible. By learning how to safely acquire Bitcoin at an exchange, you can protect your investment while you take the step of diversifying into the digital currency Bitcoin

CHAPTER 7: BITCOIN SCAM

One of the most important things to learn for anyone who is considering using the new digital currency Bitcoin is to learn about how to avoid Bitcoin scams and make sure that you are always getting what you pay for and never getting ripped off or having your money stolen. Years ago when credit cards were being accepted online as payment by merchants for the very first time, this was also the heyday of online credit card fraud because online purchasing with credit cards was such a new industry that it was impossible to address all security concerns before they led to fraud adequately.

The Same Problem Exists Today With Bitcoin

The types of scams that are being operated today using Bitcoin are eerily similar to the types of credit card scams that existed on the Internet less than 20 years ago when people started making online purchases with credit cards for the very first time. Since it is the introduction of a new payment method, the market is just getting accustomed to but is not necessarily entirely familiar with.

It is always the computer hackers and scammers that line up first to try and sucker people out of their money who are either ignorant of cyber security or who make a critical mistake that can endanger their money online.

Many Bitcoins Operators Have Been Shut Down

There are a handful of Bitcoin exchanges today that are considered reputable and have a large number of positive reviews, but there are over a dozen Bitcoin exchanges that have been shut down and no longer exist because of their shady business practices and their reluctance to implement industry standard money laundering prevention practices. Certain Bitcoin exchanges were alleged to be scams from the very beginning that were designed to prey on naive investors who did not know enough to keep their funds safe.

So if you are going to use a Bitcoin exchange today then make sure you take the time to check its reviews and establish that it is a legitimate business.

1. Malware is hidden in fake Bitcoin wallets

The nature of social media means that users click on what they perceive to be interesting links -- and the chance of an easy way of getting Bitcoin might be enough to catch some users. Cyber criminals know this and are luring Twitter users into following links which distribute malware.

Not only could users find that cyber thieves potentially compromise their details, or their device roped into the botnet, but also the cyber criminals will generate revenue from successfully luring victims into clicking these links.

The lesson here is that if an offer on social media sounds too good to be true, it usually is -- especially if it's coming from an anonymous or default account.

2. Bitcoin phishing

Cyber criminals are posing as legitimate Bitcoin services, impersonating brands to gain trust from victims. Behind these veneers of credibility are phishing websites which entice users to enter their Bitcoin keys. But once the key is entered, the hacker can freely spend from the victim's wallet.

3. Bitcoin 'flipping.'

Many people buy Bitcoin in the hope that it'll go up in value and they can make a profit by selling it at a later date. Impatient investors often turn to Bitcoin flipping schemes in the attempt to make a quick profit.

Typically, these schemes offer to increase a user's investment -- for a fee rapidly. Cybercriminals are taking advantage of this by distributing links on social media, which claim they'll flip Bitcoins, but the real intention is stealing from those naive enough to make payments via links they've found on social media.

4. Pyramid schemes

The final Bitcoin scam experiencing a spike in popularity is the classic pyramid scheme.

Cybercriminals encourage people to sign up to a scheme with a low initial investment -- then reap the rewards when they sign up new members to the scheme. It doesn't take long for hundreds of people to have handed over payment, at which point the original scammer walks away -- taking a wedge of ill-gotten Bitcoin gains with them and leaving victims out of pocket.

The total number of social media URLs sharing links to these four types of scams came to 126,276,549, say cyber security researchers at Zero FOX, with 3,618 different scams identified. The high number of scams suggests that botnets are being deployed to spread links.

Scammers, be they peddling Bitcoin or otherwise, love social media for all the same reasons modern brand marketers do. They can reach any target demographic across the globe by choosing the right hashtag, said Phil Tully, senior data scientist at Zero FOX.

"The ease of use has never been simpler, the cost has never been lower, and the power and scale have never been greater. For a cyber-criminal, it's the new superhighway for illicit activity; billions of victims, lacking security controls and uninhibited access," he added.

Bitcoin Digital Wallet Safety Tips

Securing your digital wallet where your Bitcoins are stored is of paramount importance when it comes to maintaining the integrity of your funds. If you ever reveal your Bitcoin address and you have not changed the setting on your digital wallet software to be encrypted with a private key, then it can be possible for a scammer to try and steal money directly out of your account. By taking the time to educate yourself about the potential Bitcoin scams that are out there, you can make sure that you can steer clear of those of focus only on the legitimate uses of Bitcoin as a currency.

CHAPTER 8: BITCOIN USERS

While the digital currency Bitcoin is one of the most exciting new developments in the field of personal finance and many individuals around the world are accepting it as a legitimate form of payment, it is not as secure as established major currencies such as the dollar, pound, and euro. Because Bitcoin is currently decentralized and unregulated, it can be possible to lose your Bitcoins without any possible way to recover them if you're digital Bitcoin wallet gets hacked or compromised. By following these three tips about digital wallet safety, you can be sure that you are getting the most out of your Bitcoin experience and that your investment is secure.

Protect Your Secure Password

One of the features that will come with all digital wallet software for holding Bitcoins is that you will be able to encrypt your transactions by choosing a secure password and then entering this password every time you send or receive Bitcoins. As long as you keep your password safe then nobody will be able to access your Bitcoin funds but you, thereby making your digital wallet secure from anyone gaining unauthorized access. You should make sure that your secure password is hard to guess and has a combination of letters and numbers so that it cannot be randomly guessed.

Do Not Publish Your Bitcoin Address Online

Publishing your Bitcoin address at any publicly accessible location on the internet is a very bad idea since your Bitcoin address is very similar in nature to your email address, and anyone who has it can try to take money from your digital wallet. Unless you want to accept donations into your Bitcoin account publicly, then you should always keep your Bitcoin address private, and you should also use your digital wallet software to issue a new address on a periodic basis.

Check Your Computer for Spyware

If you are going to be running digital wallet software on your computer, then you should also be running software that will check for viruses and spyware so that it can be eliminated. You should be sure that your PC with your digital wallet is spyware free because it can be possible for certain software programs to steal the sensitive data that you enter into your computer including your secure digital wallet password. While Bitcoin is still in its early adoption phase of technology, many people are diversifying into Bitcoins, and it is essential that you know how to protect your digital wallet to keep your Bitcoin investment safe.

Bitcoin has made significant progress towards becoming the world's first truly global currency over the past few years. To gain better perspective on bitcoin's impact, we took a look at global wallet downloads, demonstrated interest by region, exchange volumes across currencies, mining node locations, real-world interactions around bitcoin, and the major companies and investors pushing the bitcoin economy forward.

Bitcoin Software Downloads

We began by looking at which countries had the most downloads of Bitcoin software and then calculated the trends over time and within the context of some other factors. Worth noting: while this likely serves as a reasonable proxy, it is not inclusive of all bitcoin users, as hosted wallets, thin wallets and holdings at exchanges would not be reflected her global wallet downloads

The United States is the clear frontrunner regarding a total number of downloads. China had surprisingly few downloads for a country its size until the recent documentary aired by China's largest state-run broadcaster. As shown in the chart above and echoed elsewhere in our findings, Russia was an early adopter but has since tapered off relative to interest growing elsewhere around the globe.

To normalize for country size, we compared total wallet downloads to the population of each country to find penetration into each region. In doing so, we quickly realized the Nordic countries are the clear leaders in bitcoin adoption. As the second chart below indicates, one probable reason for this is the region's familiarity with and access to technology – all of the Nordic countries rank among the highest in the world for internet penetration.

They also all share similar and uniquely successful socioeconomic models based on a strong mutual trust between the citizens and states. So much so that Päivi Heikkinen, Finland's Head of the Division for Oversight of Financial Markets Infrastructure explicitly responded to a question about whether or not bitcoin is illegal by stating, "Not at all; people can invest in and use any money they prefer."

Historical search engine traffic from around the globe tells an interesting story as well. By tracking this, we can see the waxing and waning interest from different regions. The chart below shows interest from key countries across different time scales. The way Google Trends offers data is set by normalizing search data for population size and then assigning a value of 100 to the region with the greatest number of normalized searches. Normalized data from other regions is then compared to that on a scale of 0 to 100.

Bitcoin searches

The chart above offers some interesting information. Most notably, interest in China has grown tremendously, particularly in the last 30 days since the documentary aired. We can also see from this graph that interest from Russia has slowed, relative to other countries, and some new entrants like the Czech Republic are beginning to emerge.

Searches and software downloads show interest, but the true story unfolds when money enters the picture, so looking at exchange volumes across currencies offers even deeper insight into the evolving Bitcoin narrative.

As would be expected, USD still dominates trading volume, but mapped against other currencies we can see a consistent declining trend as other countries, and their currencies enter the picture in larger amounts.

USD as a share of total bitcoin trading volume has fallen from near 100% to approximately 80% over the past two years. The most notable gain from is from CNY (Chinese Yuan), which grew from approximately 0.4% of total volume in April 2012 to an impressive 4.7% in April 2013.

Within the still-dominant USD trading, there is a healthy trend of diversification away from Mt. Gox towards alternative exchanges. As shown in the chart below, alternative exchanges have gained traction on the DDoS-susceptible leader in the space – a trend likely to continue after their recent loss of Dwolla as an account funding source and investigation by the Department of Homeland Security. Worth noting, the chart below should be viewed as an approximation, as data for exchanges that have shut down over the years was not available for this analysis.

Connected Nodes

Bitcoin is only as strong as the network on which it is based, so the value of connected nodes cannot be overlooked in an analysis of global adoption. The chart below shows a snapshot of the geographical breakdown of connected nodes taken on May 18.

Real World Interaction

The utilization of Bitcoin in the real world, outside of the internet, will be paramount to its broader proliferation. There have been major advancements towards this, such as Kreuzberg, Berlin recently showing the world a significant step forward by deeply integrating bitcoin into the local economy and restaurants in New York City beginning to accept it as well.

As a proxy to determine the propensity for a region to bring the bitcoin movement offline, we looked at the number of people participating in bitcoin-oriented meet ups across the world. The chart below shows the number of participants in the largest meet ups in each city, grouped by country. The usual suspects are all present, with newcomers like Israel and Argentina demonstrating significant real world interest.

Breaking down offline bitcoin interest in the US even further, San Francisco and New York City remain the clear leaders, with a strong showing from Chicago and Seattle, the latter of which is home to Coin Lab, the first VC-backed Bitcoin startup in the US.

At the backbone of the bitcoin movement are a handful of visionary entrepreneurs and cautious investors. To see where the future of bitcoin is being built, we compiled a list of leading bitcoin companies and venture capitalists, focusing on the US as it has by far the greatest number of successful companies and investment capital flow to date.

The notion of international collaboration across disparate individuals has never before been achieved at this scale, outside of the internet itself. There is a bright future ahead for Bitcoin, and we're looking forward to helping it unfold.

BITCOIN CASINO PLAYER AND MEMPOOL

Bitcoin wallets are used to transfer bitcoin from one to another thus making it possible to transact in bitcoins. There are several bitcoin wallets available, and while some can be downloaded to the computer, some are clouds based. Among the various wallets available, each wallet offers its specific recommendations and benefits. The most convenient and comfortable bitcoin wallets to use are the cloud wallets, though one should remember that when one entrust the bitcoins to the cloud-based wallet, the responsibility of the BTC lies with the business holding the. Thus bringing in the vital issue of trust in cloud-based Bitcoin wallet. The most recommended cloud-based Bitcoin wallets are copied.io and bitgo.com. Alternatively, bitcoin wallets are also available as downloadable programs which are called software wallets. The user exercises absolute control over these wallets, and therefore, they are considered to be comparatively more secure than the cloud based bitcoin wallets. Some examples of software wallets are Electrum and copy.io.

The next the most commonly asked questions in bitcoin use is how to buy and sell bitcoins. To get hold of bitcoins, there are several possible ways. The most straightforward way is to purchase the bitcoins directly. This direct

BITCOIN

purchase can be made through a trusted bitcoin exchange. One of the trusted bitcoin exchange is bitsstamp.net and USD/EUR/GBP, etc. can be used to buy bitcoin. Alternatively, one can even purchase bitcoins from other individuals, around you who are willing to sell bitcoins. These face to face transactions can be conducted to procure bitcoins. Moreover, you can also search and contact bitcoin exchanges near you for secure bitcoin purchase.

Bitcoin transactions are very straightforward, and when you are purchasing something online from a store which transacts in bitcoin, they share with you the address for bitcoin transaction. They provide you with the address to which you have to send the appropriate amount of the bitcoins from your wallet. Although bitcoin transactions are instantaneous like any online transaction, the actual transfer or arrival can take up to few hours.

Bitcoins are not unlimited and have a cap of 21 million bitcoins which is the **"whole"** bitcoins. However, the inherent quality of the bitcoin is that it can be transacted even it is divided into halves, quarters, tenths and even in its smallest amount called the **"Satoshi"**. Thus there is abundant Bitcoin available for circulation.

Let us look at the five basic essential traits of bitcoin:

1. This virtual currency has no central authority overruling it. Its transactions are not governed by governments, banks and businesses, who cannot seize funds from any bitcoin user.
2. The currency is very easy to use, and transaction accounts can be easily and quickly put up as opposed to traditional accounts. Also for setting up a bitcoin wallet, no questions are fees asked.
3. It provides with blanket anonymity for conducting any transactions and allows for anonymous sale and purchase.
4. It ensures transparency through the block chain which is a public storage for information thus ensuring transparency in numbers but anonymity in accounts.

5. It is free from any fees, and thus even for the minutest of the transaction, no fee is charged.

The BitCoin Mempool is the storage area for all pending BitCoin transactions. Here's how it works. When you perform a transaction, it is first transmitted and verified by the available BitCoin nodes. Upon verification completion, it then goes into the Mempool (Memory Pool). The transaction waits in the pool until the next available BitCoin miner processes it into the next available BitCoin block.

Every node has a different rendition of the transactions waiting to be processed because these nodes have different RAM storage capacities. This also explains the different numbers of operations found within each pool.

Due to the limited RAM available for each pool, the node allocates transactions according to their size by applying a minimal fee threshold. Transactions with fees per kb that are lower than the threshold are instantly removed from the Mempool, and only new transactions with a fee per kb large enough are given access to the Mempool.

Also whenever a node gets a new valid block of transactions, it removes and processes all the transactions contained within that block from its Mempool. The Mempool size will of course sharply decrease in preparation for a new block of transactions.

The BitCoin Mempool and Bitcoin Improvement Proposals.

Bitcoin Improvement Proposals (BIPs) are the design documents created for introducing features or information to the Bitcoin protocol. These proposals are the standard way of conveying ideas since Bitcoin, being open-source, has no formal structure.

The BitCoin Mempool is a part of the BIP 35 Bitcoin Improvement Proposal. The proposal can be easily found on the Github website. This technology also helps SPV wallets (lightweight client wallets) Record and maintain transactions across the network.

BITCOIN

The BitCoin Mempool and Simplified Payment Verification.

SPV wallets play a significant role in BitCoin transactions. SPV is the acronym for "Simplified Payment Verification". This is a Bitcoin protocol feature that is usually implemented in client wallets. It allows the creation of "lightweight" bitcoin wallet clients.

These types of wallets that do not need to download the entire BitCoin Block Chain to work. This makes it possible to install an SPV wallet onto your mobile phones, tablet or any other device that has limited space.

The BitCoin Mempool vs Transaction Speed.

The overall speed of processing transactions over the network is determined by the rate of mining new blocks of transactions verses the rate of new transactions arriving into the Mempool.

If the rate of mining new blocks of transactions ever becomes lower than the rate of new transactions arriving into the Mempool, then you will have what is considered a "bottleneck" situation. In this scenario, transactions can take a longer time to get approved. This is, of course, dependent on the transaction size and the attached fee.

BitCoin Mempool Analysis.

For a visual analysis (filled with real-time charts) of the BitCoin Mempool, you can go to the BitCoin Ticker website (bitcointicker.co/networkstats/). This is one of the places where you can go to analyse the overall health of the BitCoin network.

In the charts, you can view the current Mempool size, the number of node connections, the speed of transactions, the total number of BitCoins processed and the latest transactions. Understanding the statistical data displayed is important to anyone who is interested in the world of BitCoins.

BITCOIN

BitCoins are still (relatively speaking) in the infancy stage. As technology improves, these advancements will improve the BitCoin infrastructure which will lead to even faster transactions across the BitCoin Mempool. At this current rate, there will soon come a time when BitCoin transactions can be verified almost instantly from anywhere in the world.

************END************

www.ingramcontent.com/pod-product-compliance
Lightning Source LLC
Chambersburg PA
CBHW050019230526
45470CB00003B/1041